Memoirs of a Follower

Developing the art
of listening to God
at work

MARION SANDERS

Memoirs of a Follower
Published by Marion Sanders
New Zealand
memoirsbymarion@gmail.com

ISBN 978-0-473-43659-9 (Softcover)
ISBN 978-0-473-43660-5 (ePUB)
ISBN 978-0-473-43661-2 (Kindle)

Editing & Production:
Andrew Killick
Castle Publishing Services
www.castlepublishing.co.nz

Cover illustration:
Olivia Bell

Cover design:
Paul Smith

The names of people appearing in this book
have been changed to protect their privacy.

Dedicated to
the many Christ-followers who,
over the years,
encouraged me
in my faith journey

Contents

Preface

We may ignore but we can nowhere evade, the presence of God. The world is crowded with him. He walks everywhere 'incognito'. And the incognito is not always hard to penetrate. The real labour is to remember to attend. In fact, to come awake. Still more, to remain awake.
– C.S. Lewis, *Letters to Malcolm*

~

EVEN THOUGH THE PERSONAL pronoun is used on every page of this book, the stories, or vignettes you will find here are really about God – His grace towards me, His willingness to guide me, and His patience with me as I journeyed towards a deeper understanding of how to listen to Him in my workplace.

While my stories are specific to teaching, this same grace, willingness and patience are available to anybody seeking to live their faith each day in whatever role God has entrusted to them.

I came into Christian education after a number of years teaching in the state system. I was a Christian and a qualified teacher, but I had not fully made the connection between the two. Obviously I did have some awareness of God's input in my working life, but it wasn't until I was invited to help establish a Christian school that I began to intentionally explore important differences between being a 'Christian teacher' and teaching 'Christianly'.

I was daunted by the task of contributing to the birth of a new school, but on seeking counsel from my father he reminded me, 'Opportunities like this come once in a person's lifetime… and besides… who is your helper?' It was an important reminder of the presence of God in my life. Thus encouraged, I stepped into the challenge. The school was built, and the first students arrived, and so began my adventure into a new way of teaching.

I recognised myself as a rather slow learner and so I asked God to ring bells in my head every time I thought, said or did anything that was not in line with His way of educating children. And ring those bells He did! In fact, the bells rang every day for the first few years.

It's true I grew up in a Christian family, and it's true I made an early decision to follow Jesus, but I had grown up within the state education system and had been trained in a state Teachers College. Much of what I had learned from these sources was helpful, but I had also inadvertently taken on board powerful philosophies, priorities and practices that were not in line with Biblical teaching. I had so much adjusting to do, so much rethinking of my rationale for decisions made when working with students. Yet God patiently and graciously engaged with me. Over time the bells rang less often, and less stridently, and instead I disciplined myself to listen for His still, small voice.

The vignettes in this book are drawn from the various contexts in which I've worked. Firstly there are a few stories from the days before I was involved in Christian schooling. A further set of stories is sourced from my experiences working as a primary school teacher and then principal. And lastly I share evidence of God's guidance while serving as a teacher educator, including stories related to teaching overseas.

Interspersed within the vignettes are examples of interactions with God that occurred outside these specific contexts but which influenced my understanding of what it means to be a Christian teacher. Each vignette is preceded by a quote or two which I think elaborate the focus of that story. You will also find Latin phrases scattered throughout – the result of a life-long interest sparked when I was at secondary school.

As God prompted my memory and I collected together the various stories, I noticed a theme. All are about small incidents, little moments and seemingly insignificant events. From time to time God has intervened in big ways, on occasion literally 'preserving my life', on others helping me make life-changing decisions. But when I waited on God to open my memory as I commenced writing this book, it was the small, everyday interventions He reminded me about. Perhaps there's a message in that for us all.

I became familiar with Psalm 139 at a young age. While I found much of the psalm a great comfort, I now realise that I interpreted verses seven to 10 in a rather punitive way. 'Where can I go from your Spirit? Where can I flee from your presence?' Perhaps linking them with the story of Jonah, I saw these verses as a warning that God is aware of my every move and, therefore, I needed to be careful not to disappoint Him. I now realise that this fearful 'I need to watch out' interpretation misses the point. Instead, I adopt a joyful 'He's watching over me' kind of interpretation – an awareness of the ever-present, indeed constant, loving intervention of God in my daily life, which I sincerely welcome.

We often miss noticing this constant care. We are not so good at spotting the sacred in everyday life, mainly because we're not looking or listening for it. We become too busy, hurriedly rushing from task to task, from conversation to task, to event… This way of being has been described as hurry sickness – the result of the lost art of lingering with God and with others. We trust God for eternal things, but fall back to relying on our own strength to solve our daily challenges. We thank God when major events work out, but we overlook the significance of the little things He does for us every day. When I recognise that God intervenes, I have more patience and trust in His purposes, and find more joy in daily life.

This book can be read in sequence, from cover to cover, but it would be equally appropriate for you to dip into it from time to time. Whatever approach you choose, I pray that as you read, you will want to join me in giving glory to God.

I have intentionally left empty spaces throughout this book. Feel free to use these spaces to scribble down your own thoughts and experiences. Perhaps one of my vignettes will remind you of an example of God's intervention in your own life, or perhaps you will want to meditate on a particular truth.

My testimony is that God is present with us in our vocations. He speaks to us, and for us, in the midst of our daily tasks. He challenges our thinking and our decisions, and He actively intervenes to bring about His purposes when we are alert to His leading.

I hope this book will encourage you to discover the joy of listening for God, and walking with the Spirit, in your teaching, or indeed, in whatever area of service God has called you to.

He offers to be an ever-present help. Stay awake and welcome Him!

Falling Into Teaching

For I know the plans I have for you, says the Lord. They are plans for good and not for evil, to give you a future and a hope. – Jeremiah 29:11 (TLB)

~

I CAME INTO TEACHING almost by accident.

The story began when I was completing my sixth form year (or Year 12 as it's called these days) and my father asked about my future plans. I earnestly desired to go back to school for my final year, but not for academic reasons, since I had already been accredited with University Entrance. I had recently been introduced to cricket and had become enamoured with the game – so much so that I imagined myself playing for New Zealand. The first step in that process would be staying on for seventh form and playing in the school's top team. When I shared this idea with my father, he quickly, but gently, informed me that he could not afford to keep me in school for another year just so I could play sport.

Hopes dashed, I began to think of other options. I was undecided. Opportunities probably existed to venture into a wide range of occupations, but I recall limiting my choices to nursing, social work or teaching. I was still trying to decide, when it was announced at school assembly that an interview panel from the local Teachers College would be visiting the next week, to speak with prospective students.

This news provided an easy way to settle my conundrum. So without further thought, I added my name to the list of interviewees. I was still only 16 but was offered a place in the three-year primary teacher training programme, which I accepted.

There appeared to be little thought in my decision. In retrospect though it became obvious that this was God's chosen path for me. As a five-year-old I stood on the front porch shouting out encouragement to passers-by to come to church. As a seven-year-old I organised my own club, which met weekly in our garage for several years. It was a highly-organised, well-structured and carefully-recorded gathering, which included 'home' activities and guest speakers, as well as ventures into the great outdoors. Each session always began with the roll being taken!

In Brownies I was a sixer and in Guides I was a patrol leader. In my early teens I led a group of Christian children in weekly discipleship meetings and fulfilled leadership roles within church services. God was giving me many opportunities to not only develop my leadership skills but, in particular, to experience the joy of helping others learn.

From one perspective it could be said that I fell into teaching, but it is probably more accurate to say God led me there.

Love

God is love. When we take up permanent residence in a life of love, we live in God and God lives in us. This way, love has the run of the house, becomes at home and matures in us, so that we're free of worry on Judgment Day – our standing in the world is identical with Christ's. There is no room in love for fear. Well-formed love banishes fear. Since fear is crippling, a fearful life is one not yet fully formed in love. We, though, are going to love – love and be loved. First we were loved, now we love. He loved us first. If anyone boasts, 'I love God,' and goes right on hating his brother or sister, thinking nothing of it, he is a liar. If he won't love the person he can see, how can he love the God he can't see? The command we have from Christ is blunt: Loving God includes loving people. You've got to love both.
– 1 John 4:18-21 (MSG)

I BEGAN MY OFFICIAL journey into teaching as a 16-year-old and had my initial practicum experience in a school where many students exhibited challenging behaviour. My first few days were spent observing the junior class, and I noticed a particular student whose behaviour was extreme, whose manner was rude and whose body odour was often unpleasant. I worried that I would be unable to connect with this boy (whom we'll call 'Jim') in any meaningful way. I secretly hoped he would not be in any of the groups with which I was asked to work.

On this practicum, student teachers in my year were assigned various tasks, including working with one group of children in reading, another group in writing and another in maths. We were also asked to take an aspect of the arts with a small group, and I had chosen music.

After a few days of initiation, my associate teacher assigned me to my groups. To my consternation I discovered that Jim was in every single one! This meant I would be interacting with him multiple times every day. (In hindsight I think maybe the associate teacher was using my presence in the classroom to give herself a much-needed break.)

I went home feeling distraught, concerned that Jim's conduct might affect my ability to pass the requirements of the practicum. I was unsure how to handle his behaviour. I had observed adults working with difficult children before – my father had managed a boys' home – but in this situation I felt completely out of my depth.

Although I wasn't yet fully acquainted with Christian teaching concepts, I already knew that relationship was essential, and that the foundation of relationship was love. But how could I love this child who seemed so unlovable? I earnestly asked God for an answer. His reply was so simple but, to a 16-year-old, also very profound.

'I want you to love Jim with my love. See him with my eyes.

Listen to him with my ears. Respond to him with my heart. Offer him acceptance, joy and hope.'

I spent the next five weeks beginning each day with a heartfelt prayer, asking God to help me love Jim with His love, then practised the instructions God subsequently gave me. I tried to see Jim as God would see him, to listen to Jim the way God would listen, to accept him warmly and to actively look for the marks of God's gifts in this little man's life. Obeying God's directions changed my focus from fear to hope, inadequacy to confidence, from noticing deficits to celebrating strengths, and from distaste to delight.

By the end of the practicum, I not only loved Jim with God's love, I also felt genuine personal love towards him. We had become 'best mates' and I was sad to say goodbye. He even offered me a farewell gift of a small broken toy that he brought from home. Jim had taught me so much, and hopefully I had also taught him things of lasting value in his troubled life. What a gracious act of God this situation had turned out to be!

Deus caritas est
(God is love)

The Rut Breaker

Don't copy the behaviour and customs of this world, but be a new and different person with a fresh newness in all you do and think. Then you will learn from your own experience how his ways will really satisfy you.
– Romans 12:2 (TLB)

I AM INDEBTED TO ALL the teachers who, over the years, allowed me to observe their practice – even those whose teaching styles I didn't want to emulate. Many of my most strongly-held beliefs about my personal responsibilities as a teacher have stemmed from early experiences as a student teacher.

One classroom I visited for several weeks was led by an older teacher, Mr X, who was very accomplished, very warm towards me and very accommodating in letting me try my hand at whatever I wanted to explore in terms of curriculum.

The students respected him and his classroom ran smoothly. I don't recall any blips in the behaviour of the children, and I was learning a lot about management. As a 'serious' student I obcyed the instruction of my Teachers College tutor and, early in the placement, asked if I could see Mr X's planning.

'I don't have any written planning. I have been teaching the same class level for 40 years now and I know exactly what I am going to teach each day of the year. You can test me out if you like!' he told me.

His statement stunned me. It explained why the students, although well-behaved, demonstrated so little engagement and passion for their learning. I also understood why the children had so enthusiastically made use of the percussion instruments during my music lessons!

Even though I was still very young and only just beginning my journey as a teacher, I somehow sensed that this man's approach was not one I wanted to emulate – even though he seemed quite chuffed with his achievement. I immediately decided not to allow myself to stay in the same class level for consecutive years, so as to avoid getting into a rut – a resolve I was able to follow for most of my career.

As time passed, God showed me the importance of being responsive to each new group of students with whom I worked. The ability to modify, adapt and change units of work (i.e. approaches, strategies, content and product) is an essential skill for effective teaching – especially when we strive to recognise the *imago dei* (image of God) in each student.

A wise teacher makes learning a joy, and a student's passionate engagement in learning is only possible when we ourselves are passionate about what we are teaching. Ruts narrow our vision.

Rocky Road is Not Always Tasty

Courage doesn't always roar. Sometimes courage is the quiet voice at the end of the day saying, 'I will try again tomorrow.' – Mary Anne Radmacher

~

My first year as an 18-year-old beginning teacher proved to be a rocky road – despite graduating with distinction from Teachers College. Because I had been given a government-sponsored allowance during my three years of training, I was bonded to teach at allocated state schools for a further three years. Thus, for the first year I found myself placed in a small suburban school in the Wellington area, teaching seven-year-olds.

I entered this important stage of my journey with great excitement, but soon came up against the realities of the situation. To start with, my principal believed that, since I had just graduated and was up with the latest developments, I would be the ideal person to completely rewrite the school's curriculum documents.

As it was a small school, the principal had been unable to handpick my class. Thus, among my first students was a young man, whose frequent anger explosions one day led to his pulling a knife on me, and a young lady so emotionally disturbed she only ever painted in red. My principal did little to support me in these challenges, simply pointing out to me that when he entered my room, he could make the children quieten without even speaking. He was a very tall man, quite imposing, and carried an air of authority. He didn't seem to recognise the advantages he had over me, a novice teacher who stood at just over five feet!

I gradually won over the class through music, art, sport and drama – as well as engaging in literacy and numeracy! I felt we were 'ticking along' nicely. Then came the bombshell. At that time, teachers in their first year were observed for half a day by a member of the Board of Education inspectorate. My visit resulted in the inspector declaring that I was in the wrong career – that I was clearly not cut out to be a teacher and that I should seriously consider leaving. This verdict certainly led to a degree of self-doubt, and great chagrin, given the determined effort and sacrificial time I had put into building classroom community. To his credit, my principal finally showed proactive support by challenging this appraisal and asking for another inspector to provide a second opinion.

This next lengthy inspection was highly successful – so successful in fact that when I told the second visitor that, as part of being bonded, I was being placed for my second year at a school in a central North Island town I had never heard of, he responded, 'Just say the word and I'll arrange to have you stay here in this area.'

The offer was very tempting, and occupied my thoughts for several days. But as I pondered and prayed, I realised that I could not accept. After regularly praying for a number of months that

God would direct my future path, to take the inspector's offer would be an admission that I believed God had 'got it wrong'. I needed to trust Him.

I declined the offer, completed my year, and headed north. In that unknown town I had many wonderful teaching experiences, became involved in community initiatives, and met my future husband – a banker who had been posted to the same town because of a clerical spelling error! God had everything in control.

In virtute
(Have courage)

No Rabbits Here

I'm not ashamed to own my Lord,
or to defend his cause,
maintain the glory of his cross,
and honour all his laws.
– Isaac Newton (1642-1727)

I WAS STILL A newbie to teaching (in my second year) and was a brand new staff member at a big school in a construction town. I was blessed to be placed in charge of a class of 42 students, mostly boys. I settled quickly and enjoyed all my interactions with parents, staff and children.

Easter was approaching and the other teachers began to talk excitedly together. It became obvious they were planning an annual Easter event, and it was also obvious that everyone assumed everyone else would participate. However, the event provided me with an ethical dilemma and I struggled with how to respond. You see, on the Thursday before Easter an adult-sized rabbit would be hopping from class to class depositing Easter eggs.

I wasn't against Easter eggs as such, but I did feel uncomfortable about the mode of delivery. I was a firm believer in the idea that such things as the Easter bunny drew attention away from the true meaning of the holiday. I knew there were protocols around just how much of the biblical Easter message I could share within the classroom. I also knew, though, that I didn't want to reinforce the secular Easter stories! What should I do? I summoned up courage and spoke to the principal.

I explained my dilemma and asked permission to have the rabbit bypass my class. My children would still get an Easter egg, from me, along with a discussion about the symbolic meaning of the sweet treat in relation to new life and the Easter story.

After some discussion he agreed. For the first time since beginning teaching, I had made a public declaration of faith within my school setting.

Admittedly, there were one or two children who looked out with longing eyes as the rabbit hopped passed our room, but most of the students were content with the way we shared Easter together. I had stayed true to my beliefs and to the One I follow.

Sectare fidem
(Hold firm to the faith)

A Joyful Song

We tend to use prayer as a last resort, but God wants it to be our first line of defence. We pray when there's nothing else we can do, but God wants us to pray before we do anything at all. – Oswald Chambers

~

EARLY ON IN MY career, I had the privilege of working with a five-year-old child who experienced a number of learning challenges, along with serious physical disabilities. She faced these difficulties with good humour, determination and a maturity beyond her years. With her walking frame she ventured wherever her classmates went, and with her teacher aide alongside her she focused on completing manual tasks.

But she so wanted to learn how to read. I tried various strategies, talked with colleagues and gathered information. Nothing seemed to harness her pronounced stutter, which affected her fluency and therefore limited comprehension. Her disappointment was very obvious and our reading sessions together caused her to become really frustrated. I was committed to helping her achieve her goal, but I had reached the end of my limited repertoire.

Finally, in desperation, I begged God for a strategy to aid this precious child.

What was His advice?

'Sing the stories. Sing each page. Make up tunes but sing the words contained in the book.'

So sing we did. The melody-making seemed like a game to her. Our focus was so strongly on the song, that the words began to flow smoothly and understanding grew. A smile replaced the frustration. Our reading times became joy-filled excursions into the world of books.

I gave thanks to God and determined that in future prayer would be my first thought, not my last resort.

Proving God's Presence

Have I not commanded you? Be strong and courageous! Do not be terrified or dismayed (intimidated), for the Lord *your God is with you wherever you go.'* – Joshua 1:9 (AMP)

~

I temporarily left teaching to care for my growing family. After an eight-year break, I ventured back into the classroom, by way of relief teaching.

Being placed with a new group of students every day certainly grows a teacher's management skills and hones relational abilities. In this environment, my strategies became sharper, my ability to connect was strengthened and my flexibility and adaptability were enhanced. Relief teaching demands responsiveness and quick decision-making, which is helped when the teacher is able to draw on tacit knowledge. Additionally, I found that relieving in a number of schools built my sense of teacher identity, and confidence in my ability to work with a wide age range.

Most of my relief teaching experiences were enjoyable. With

multiple visits to some schools, I soon built rapport within the staffroom, and my feelings of uncertainty became less common as time passed.

However, there was one school that always caused me a degree of internal tension. This large intermediate usually required a bevy of relievers each day. After being called early in the morning, we would assemble in the staffroom, waiting for the deputy principal to assign our respective roles.

Most classes were easily managed, but there was one class we were all hesitant about. Fortunately, the class teacher, a mature experienced male, was seldom absent. But one Monday morning, we were informed that he was going to be absent for the next three days.

We waited anxiously to see who had been chosen for the daunting role of supervising his class. The deputy principal acknowledged that it would be a challenging assignment and offered to create a roster of relievers who would swap each half day. He announced which two relievers would be assigned for the first day. I was relieved (excuse the pun) when I wasn't named. On Tuesday I also managed to 'escape' selection. On Wednesday another teacher was given the task of managing the class for the morning, and as I was just about to breathe a prayer of thanks, believing I would miss out this time, my name was announced as the afternoon supervisor.

My initial response was one of disbelief – even fear. The day before, one of the relievers had left the classroom in tears. How would I manage this rebellious group of 12-year-olds? But then I chastised myself. Why should I be afraid when God had promised to be with me? Did I really believe these promises or was it just talk? I determined to put faith into action and adopted a plan.

During the lunch break I went into the classroom and prayed a simple prayer. 'Lord, I need your help. I feel inadequate for what lies ahead. Please, when I speak, I want to speak with your authority.' Next, I wrote on the blackboard assigned reading tasks for the afternoon. I was careful to word these items with clarity and to ensure the level of understanding required was suitable for the age group. When the bell rang, I stood at the door and silently prayed over each student as they entered the classroom. I asked God to fill the children with His peace – to quieten their hearts and still their bodies.

I walked to the front of the room and quietly spoke. 'Your work for this afternoon is on the board. I am sure you will find it both interesting and straightforward. I want this work to be done in silence. You may start.'

That was all I said, and the instructions were actually followed. The class worked in silence! After 40 minutes, one young man became a little restless. I stood behind him, prayed silently, and he settled. The entire afternoon passed without a word being spoken and everyone completed the work. Before I knew it, it was the end of the day and time to pack up.

What I experienced that afternoon was nothing to do with me, or my skill as a teacher, or my charisma in the classroom. What I experienced was entirely God's doing. It was first-hand evidence of His supernatural intervention on my behalf, as a result of committing the situation to Him in prayer.

When I told a friend what had happened, she wondered how the students would have described that afternoon from their point of view. For me it was life-changing. I realised I didn't need to fear any situation that might come my way as a teacher or, indeed, in my life as a whole.

Devotions

The Lord *came and stood there, calling as at other times, 'Samuel, Samuel!' Then Samuel said, 'Speak* Lord *for your servant is listening.'* – 1 Samuel 3:10 (NIV)

~

I have long believed that children have access to God through all the same avenues that are open to adults – including the gifts of the Spirit. To this end, when I started teaching new entrants in a Christian school, we always started our day together the same way. The five-year-olds and I would sing a ditty…

Be very quiet now.
Listen to God
Thank you, God, for loving us.
Thank you, God.

After a time of silence I would invite the children to share what God had said to them. Most times they would recall the Bible story currently being studied, with responses like 'God told Noah to build the ark', or they might comment on the day, or speak out common phrases such as 'God loves you and me' or 'God made everything'.

I admit to becoming a tad despondent as the days passed and so, one morning, as we were exercising our quiet time I silently confessed my disappointment to God, and reaffirmed my certainty that He *could* speak to children too, not just adults.

I gathered the attention of the class, and once again elicited reports of God's conversations with them. The content was as usual until one boy said, 'God told me He can speak to children too, not just adults!' He spoke the exact words I had voiced in my own silent exchange with God.

I was overwhelmed by God's graciousness in that moment. I also had a whiff of His sense of humour. With great expectation I continued our morning devotional tradition.

Deus est fidelis
(God is faithful)

Staying Sane

You will keep in perfect peace all who trust in you, all whose thoughts are fixed on you! – Isaiah 26:3 (NLT)

We can be certain that God will give us the strength and resources we need to live through any situation in life that he ordains. The will of God will never take us where the grace of God cannot sustain us. – Billy Graham

~

A COLLEAGUE CASUALLY ASKED me one day, 'How do you keep your sanity, Marion? We all know that we need time to ourselves to keep sane – to have time out doing the things we enjoy. You seem to do so many things, pack so much into a day. How do you look after yourself? How do you schedule your other pursuits? How do you get time to do things just for you?'

I was nodding assent to my colleague's philosophy on life, even as bells began to ring in my head. Why were they ringing? What he said seemed to make perfect sense. After all, isn't it true that we all need to plan times of rest and recreation?

But I had heard the bells and so over the next few days I waited before God, asking Him to clarify why He was drawing my attention to this issue. He led me to think about Jesus. I realised that Jesus often took Himself off for time alone, away from the disciples, away from the crowds. Did that prove my colleague's point? Then I remembered that when Jesus 'departed from them' it was always to spend time with His Father – to listen, to share, to meditate, to be replenished spiritually.

So that was the first key to a sane life – giving adequate time to prayer. But what about my need for rest, time out, refreshment? God drew my attention to the word 'need' and the promise in His Word that He would 'supply all my needs' – including those that I haven't even recognised yet.

It became a game – spotting the times when He provided for my need for downtime, even when I hadn't planned it; such times as finding the doctor running late with his appointments, or road works leaving me waiting in the car for five minutes, or when a parent who had requested a meeting had not yet arrived, or... Instead of being frustrated with such events, I began to welcome them as God's intervention. I became aware of so many instances where He graciously provided interludes and met my need for time out.

I still plan weekends away, or evenings out with friends, and I try to keep a Sabbath rest, but since that conversation with God, attending to personal relaxation in order to preserve my sanity has never been an urgent or over-riding preoccupation. My time is in God's hands. He is faithful and He keeps His promises.

Deus scit
(God knows)

Meeting Alan

'Who makes mouths?' Jehovah asked him. 'Isn't it I, the Lord?... Now go ahead and do as I tell you, for I will help you to speak well, and I will tell you what to say.'
– Exodus 4:11a, 12 (TLB)

ALAN STARTED SCHOOL, a tall boy for his age, neatly presented in sweet-smelling, freshly-ironed clothes, and hair brushed in place. His lunchbox bore evidence of loving preparation.

But he was like a whirlwind – a five-year-old with incredible energy, willpower and angst. He seemed to rage against the world, and me, his teacher, in particular. With a mixture of antagonism and doubtful intent, he would eyeball me from where he sat across the table.

'I'm going to send a lion to get you,' Alan would intone, through hardened jaw, his eyes glaring. This boy was the most challenging child I had taught up to that point, and his interactions with his classmates mirrored those with me. He needed strong guidance, firm expectations and prayerful responses. His behaviour forced me to draw on divine wisdom as I tried to help him, all the while sheltering the other students from his aggressive actions.

As the weeks went by, it came time for parent-teacher interviews. What would I say to Alan's parents? I always tried to speak truthfully, but how would my report be received? I was unsure how to broach the subject of their son's behaviour.

I was still deliberating as the couple stepped into the room. Without further thought I found myself saying, 'I want you to know I think you are wonderful parents.'

I was surprised by my own words. It was truly my view, but not really what I had intended to say to them, nor what I had been rehearsing in my mind.

I was equally surprised by their response. The mother began to weep, saying it was the first time anyone had endorsed her parenting. Instead she was always criticised for her son's behaviour, as if she was to blame. She was genuinely grateful for my affirmation, and this opened the door for rich dialogue.

Although they openly acknowledged that they were not Christians, Alan's parents readily responded to my offer to pray for, over and with their son. They also revealed more of their son's history, so I had a deeper understanding of the spiritual influences at play in the situation.

Afterwards, as I reflected on the conversation, I recognised that God had orchestrated the situation in such a way that it was the parent who had brought up the issue of behaviour, not me!

This encounter strengthened my heart, built trust with the parents and gave me a renewed commitment to nurture the child.

A Determined Dinosaur

Whatever is true, whatever is noble, whatever is right, whatever is pure, whatever is lovely, whatever is admirable – if anything is excellent or praiseworthy – think about such things. – Philippians 4:8 (NIV)

~

OPENING A NEW SCHOOL is a significant undertaking that involves many decisions. I was part of a team that was considering options for a literacy curriculum.

At that time, 'whole language' approaches were strongly endorsed by educational leaders and researchers, and most instructional reading materials were based on these premises. In a nutshell, the emphasis was on the reader bringing meaning to the text by predicting possible interpretations, rather than decoding the text. I knew there were many helpful aspects to this method, but as I waited on God, read literature and spoke to colleagues, I had a growing sense that something was amiss. In its core philosophy, the whole language approach seemed to have ignored foundational biblical principles about teaching and learning.

I was still new to critiquing teaching philosophies from a biblical perspective, but I immediately saw that encouraging children to simply predict words while reading, and to commend them for a 'good guess' even if incorrect, was not an honest way to guide their literacy development. The letters C.A.T will always spell cat, not kitten or moggy. Therefore those of us setting up the new school decided to use a 'structured-sequential' approach (commonly called phonics). This involved almost pedantically instilling the keys to reading and writing, gently correcting when errors occurred and encouraging perseverance, self-discipline and teachability in the children. We did this, not because it was the 'in thing', but because we believed it was the truth-filled way to develop literacy skills.

Our approach wasn't always well-received. A literacy advisor who visited us in the early days, stated that pointing out errors would damage the children's confidence. I replied that when correction is offered within a culture of loving relationship, students will develop trust in their teacher and appreciate the teacher's honesty. The advisor called me a 'dinosaur' and predicted that our school would struggle to gain students because parents would not agree with our teaching methods. He asserted he wouldn't be surprised if our school was closed within a year.

As the advisor predicted, some parents were initially unsure. One father approached the principal to voice his concerns about the slow progress his son was making in reading and writing compared to cousins of the same age attending other schools. I felt despondent when this information was relayed to me. However, immediately after hearing about the father's visit, I met another parent in the car park who commended me enthusiastically for her child's literacy progress. I thanked God for this gracious encouragement.

Over time, I understood the apparent enigma. The reading books available through the Ministry of Education were developed for a whole language approach. Therefore books for early readers were highly repetitive, aiding prediction which, in turn, produced seemingly quick progress through the early stages. However, as reading difficulty increased, prediction alone was not enough to support the reader, and progress slowed.

The structured-sequential approach showed a different trajectory. Progress was slower in the early stages, but once the truthful keys to unlocking literacy were established, confidence and competence in reading and writing quickly progressed.

Perhaps I was a dinosaur ahead of my time! Many New Zealand schools now use an amalgam of whole language and structured-sequential approaches, and the publisher who once declared to me that producing phonics material would only be 'over my dead body' now offers these books as one of the most profitable areas of the business. Incidentally, our school did not close within a year, and is still in existence 30 years later.

A related story involves a young teenager who enrolled at our school with a reading level well below that expected for his age. He really struggled with the secondary school curriculum and teaching methods. When I became aware of his situation, I offered to work with him for 30 minutes each morning.

The Ministry of Education secondary advisor severely chastised me for taking this course of action. He claimed I would damage the student's 'self-esteem', since withdrawing him from class would make him feel different to his classmates.

'This student already feels different to the rest of his class,' I responded. 'He cannot read the work in the text book or on the board. He cannot complete his homework without parental help. He knows his literacy skills are insufficient to 'make the grade'. Withdrawing him for literacy instruction has shown him we care about him as an individual of worth, and as a student with potential to learn once he masters the keys.'

The advisor wasn't convinced, but within three months no further withdrawal sessions were needed. The student was reading and writing at a level commensurate with his age. He was enjoying school, secure in the knowledge that he mattered to us.

Deus est veritas
(God is truth)

Getting to the Heart of the Matter

The Lord *does not look at the things people look at. People look at the outward appearance, but the* Lord *looks at the heart.* – 1 Samuel 16:7 (NIV)

Create in me a pure heart, O God, and renew a steadfast spirit within me. – Psalm 51:10 (NIV)

~

In my introduction, I mentioned the influence of my immersion in the state education system on my teaching philosophies, priorities and practices. One such philosophy was highlighted when a lad named Jason joined my class. He was unable to sit still, unable to focus for even a few minutes and his off-task behaviour regularly distracted the other children.

Shortly after his arrival, I completed an observation of his behaviour and noted he had interrupted the whole class 15 times in 10 minutes. I knew something had to change.

My Teachers College training had taught me about management strategies based on behaviourist theory. This approach emphasised rewards and punishment as a way of training students towards desired dispositions and habits.

I knew Jason was fascinated by computers, so I hatched a plan that involved requiring him to stay in his seat for a designated period of time, after which he would be rewarded with the opportunity to use the computer. He responded positively to the idea. Whenever I observed him quietly doing his work, I would put a tick on his chart. Once he had 10 marks he could go to the computer for 10 minutes.

This arrangement had an immediate effect. Jason had no difficulty remaining in his workplace, and quickly earned his ten marks. He went into the side room to work on the computer while I congratulated myself on the success of my plan. After 10 minutes I asked him to come back into the classroom. This he did, and, in less than 30 seconds, disrupted the whole class!

Of course, by this time bells were ringing in my head! As I questioned God, the quiet thought that came to my mind was, 'It's not the outward behaviour that needs to be changed. It's his heart. Work on the heart!'

Work on the heart? Surely only God can change a heart. But as I pondered this thought I realised that I could commit to praying for Jason, since prayer achieves much. I could model patience, care, joy and faithfulness. I could develop helpful routines, clear, well-articulated expectations and, yes, I could offer rewards – but only as a supporting strategy, not as the main approach, and only in a way that did not disadvantage or overlook those children who were always on task.

This little incident initiated a further incremental change to my classroom management practices, as God continued to patiently build on what He was teaching me.

Humility and Strength

The children of God,
those who open their lives to you
portray the wonder
and the beauty of Your Spirit.
– Leslie Brandt, *Psalms Now*

~

SHE JOINED MY CLASS – an 11-year-old sojourner, planning to spend two years at our school before returning to her home city. Her parents, so the story went, honoured her belief that God was telling her to come to our school, and so she found board, was kitted out in a new uniform and appeared at my classroom door.

She seemed so quiet, almost painfully so, seldom participating in class discussions and slow to volunteer, literally as quiet as a mouse. I found myself moving into my usual teacher mode. How can I entice her to be more collaborative? What will ease her into talking more readily? Why is she so reclusive?

But even as I considered these questions I heard God's prompting:

'What gives you the right to change a child's personality, to change the way I made her?'

Thus cautioned, I pulled back and gave her space. I welcomed her contributions when they were offered but didn't force the issue when she chose to be silent.

When the first parent-teacher evening of the year came round, the girl's mother and father travelled to be there. With sincere emotion, they thanked me for being the first of their child's teachers to allow her to 'be' – to be herself, to be reserved, to be self-contained. I thanked God for His instruction to me.

Over the months, the hidden calibre of this young lady emerged. She didn't speak very often, but when she did, the class listened because they knew her words would be insightful, thoughtful and true. She exhibited a strong, sustaining faith, and was certain of her call to our school. She formed several close friendships, and at a parents' evening she played a trombone solo with great gusto.

It takes a certain inner strength to play the trombone!

Sit laus Deo
(Thanks be to God)

Worth the Wait

There is a right time for everything... a time to be quiet and a time to speak up. – Ecclesiastes 3:1, 7b (TLB)

For God is at work within you, helping you want to obey him, and then helping you do what he wants. – Philippians 2:13 (TLB)

~

IT IS EASY FOR a teacher to be overly talkative. I often need God to quieten my tongue, and to moderate my interactions. It's so easy to jump in, to add my point of view, or respond on assumption rather than clear facts. Most importantly, if I lack discretion I can interfere with what God is teaching a student.

One such occasion occurred when I was responsible for a group of five-year-olds. Our school roll was rapidly expanding and, in the last term of the year, I found myself teaching the new entrants, temporarily housed in a small room in the middle of the secondary school.

This unusual arrangement meant that the classroom furniture

was a mixture of big people's tables and other furniture more appropriate to the age and stage of my class. I pushed most of the big tables into a corner and used them as a place to store a variety of art and craft materials. All kinds of bric-a-brac found its way under and onto this storage area.

One day I noticed a child sorting through some of these treasures. She seemed particularly interested in a pile of ribbons and lace. I watched as she laid them in a line, apparently seeking to colour coordinate as she went. Then she surreptitiously placed these under her jersey and exited the room, into the foyer where the school bags were kept.

I planned to challenge her about her actions when she returned to the classroom – to point out to her that taking these items without asking was in fact stealing, and tell her that I was disappointed she couldn't be trusted. But I felt a need to pause – to withhold my comment – and so I kept quiet.

Ten minutes later I observed the same child leave the room, and then, upon her return, gingerly return the ribbon and lace back to the materials table. She had obviously been wrestling with her actions and, of her own accord, had reached an admirable conclusion, without my needing to challenge her.

This time I did call her to me. I commended her decision-making, and her willingness to listen to her conscience. My initial silence meant that instead of just pointing out her wrong-doing, I was able to celebrate her right actions, and I hadn't usurped the role of the Holy Spirit.

Deus ducibus
(God guides)

Curriculum Choices

All children are artists and it is an indictment on our culture that so many lose their creativity, their unfettered imaginations as they grow older. – Madeleine L'Engle, *Walking on Water*

~

I'M A SLOW LEARNER but God, in His graciousness, continued to 'ring bells' in my head, teaching me and guiding me towards more effective ways of educating His cherished children. I gradually learned the art of hearing His perspective for the small choices of day-to-day interactions, as well as the major decisions affecting school-wide curriculum planning.

One morning I was walking along 'The Way' – the central footpath through our school – when a burst of inspiration popped into my head then stayed in my heart. The idea was to establish a weekly school-wide observational drawing session, and it wasn't a notion I had ever entertained before. Classes from new entrant to Year 6 would be encouraged to spend 30 minutes each week completing drawings of a variety of objects, both natural and manufactured.

I presented the idea to staff, and even though I couldn't outline the educational rationale for the approach at that time, they readily agreed to adopt the practice. At the end of the term, the benefits of the programme would be assessed.

Our discussions after 10 weeks of implementation yielded an A4 page of identified benefits, covering cognitive, social, physical and spiritual developmental areas. I think we were all surprised by the breadth and depth of these outcomes, but of course we shouldn't have been, since God has a unique view on strategies that enable effective education.

Encouraged, we continued with observational drawing as a regular component of our teaching programme.

Today, the benefits of observational drawing are more widely known, and it has become a popular part of various primary school curricula.

Too Many Coincidences

But most of all I give thanks, praise and honour to my Lord, Jesus Christ, without whom I can do no good thing and from whom all true things emanate. He is my macro-supervisor, the instigator of my passion for education, the inspirer of my desire to help develop committed, transformative teachers who truly connect with those they teach. – Acknowledgement in my doctoral thesis

~

When I had finished my Master's research I declared an end to my formal study! I had taken academic education-focused papers every year since graduating from Teachers College, but completing this particular qualification, while working full-time, caring for a family and contributing to church and community initiatives, had taken much self-discipline and sacrifice. My husband concurred. While he, my daughters and our 'extras' were incredibly supportive, the hours of seclusion had exacted a toll on family life, and so we were all content with the decision.

Imagine my surprise then, when one morning I awoke with

a burning desire to do a doctorate! I tentatively shared this with my husband, who replied, 'This is such a change of attitude that it can only mean one thing. God wants you to do more study. You must obey. Somehow we'll find the money to cover your fees.' We anticipated these would be in the vicinity of $50,000 and, since we had no savings, our decision was definitely a step of faith.

Through a fellow New Zealander, I learned of a Christian academic at Macquarie University in Sydney, Australia, who might be willing to act as my supervisor. The choice of Macquarie was also influenced by the fact that a conference speaker I had heard several times was the Director of Christian Studies there. I wasn't intending to enrol with his department, but the knowledge that this inspiring man could perhaps contribute in some way to my study was influential in my final decision. My heart seemed set on Macquarie and so I travelled to Australia to make the necessary inquiries.

The aforementioned professor did agree to supervise me, and we quickly established a rapport. The first day on campus I saw the respected conference speaker. He passed by me as he walked up some steps, but I hesitated to speak to him as he seemed to be on a mission, with a heavy briefcase and arms loaded with books.

The next day I went to the Christian Studies office, hoping to meet him there, only to learn that the previous day he had retired and had actually been in the process of leaving the campus when I had seen him. However, the new director was very welcoming and, during our conversation, casually mentioned a book by the theologian Miroslav Volf (*Exclusion and Embrace*), which became a foundational component of my study.

I proceeded through the university formalities, including a lengthy enrolment procedure. It was only as I completed all the paper work and inquired about fees, that I learned there would be no fees attached to my enrolment! At that time the Australian Government covered the fees of any doctoral work involving original research, *and* at that time the Australian government included New Zealanders in the mandate. Furthermore the university would provide me with an allowance each year to assist my study. This allowance funded my return flights to Australia for semi-regular visits to the university.

When I had been completing my Master's research a few years earlier, an Australian academic had been invited by my tutor to offer critique on my thesis prior to final submission. This generous man had then also helped me prepare an article for publication and given feedback on my first ever academic conference presentation, in Chicago. Unknown to me, his family lived within 15 minutes of Macquarie University and when they heard of my intention to study again, they opened their home to me each time I visited. God was weaving together all that was necessary for me to study.

During my university visits I continued to be aware of His guiding hand in little ways, but one instance was quite remarkable. I always worked very full days while I was in Australia, either talking with my supervisor, writing, or reading in the library. On the last day of one such visit, I had so much still to achieve, in terms of reading titles I had identified as being helpful to my study. However, I knew locating all these books and gleaning from the contents was going to be a huge task, especially as the items were scattered throughout the multi-level library.

That morning, I uttered a hurried prayer of urgency as I entered the building. I used the catalogue to find all the call numbers and set out to locate the first book. I found it, standing alongside all the other books on my list! Every single one! They were sharing the same shelf, even though they all had different call numbers. Either some other student had required exactly the same set of texts and had lazily left them on the shelf, or…?!

I once had a minister who described coincidences as 'God acting anonymously'. These anonymous acts have occurred so frequently in my life that I could never call them mere coincidences.

I always prayed about when to visit Australia, but on one occasion I arrived at the university to find that none of the computers in my department were working, my research library assistant was on holiday and my supervisor was on bereavement leave. I wondered if I had made a mistake this time, and as I asked this question of God I felt Him say, 'And who is your supervisor, Marion? You need an earthly supervisor to take you through the processes but I am supervising your learning. Trust me.'

This truth stuck with me throughout my study, and in my doctoral thesis I was able to wholeheartedly acknowledge God as my macro-supervisor.

Practise What You Preach

A young white boy, on arriving home from school, asked his mother, 'Can my friend come to play tomorrow?' His mother enquired, 'Is your friend black?' to which the young white boy replied, 'I don't know. I'll ask him tomorrow.' – Heard at a conference, original source unknown

~

A NUMBER OF YEARS ago, I was in Chicago to present a paper at the American Education Research Association conference. At that stage I hadn't travelled much, so it was a great adventure. My first morning in Chicago, I left the train station and looked for a taxi, as I was unsure where to find the conference hotel. As I walked towards the taxi rank, I noticed the first cab was being driven by a large black man. I slowed my step and looked quickly along the taxi rank to see who else was available.

Suddenly I checked myself in disbelief. Here I was, a proponent of equality of all races, hesitating to go in a taxi with a black man. I was appalled by my own behaviour and deliberately headed to that first taxi, chastising myself as I went.

I reflected on this incident at length. What had caused my reaction? Why had my emotional response been different to my cognitive beliefs? I knew this impulse was unacceptable in God's eyes. I knew my response was counter to what I would encourage others to do. Did my heart and head match and, if not, why not?

I have always known that if I'm not alert, my thoughts and feelings can be inadvertently affected by the society in which I live. This incident was an example of the power of the media – particularly newspapers, television and movies, where at that time black men were often cast as villains. My view of the world was being shaped by my sometimes careless attitude to messages that were being powerfully transmitted. These messages had created a painful discrepancy within me. I certainly didn't believe in white racial superiority but on this occasion I was avoiding contact with other races.

The opportunity to experience a new culture increases the need for reflection. For reflection to take place, I need to notice, to enquire, to be receptive to facing difficult realisations about myself and my interactions with others.

This is a continuing journey, and God has had to call me to task on a number of occasions – another example is found in the next story.

Ut diligatis invicem
(Love one another)

Beautiful Before God

There is a need to verify in praxis what we know in consciousness. – bell hooks

Faith without works is dead. – James 2:26 (TLV)

We must lay before Him what is in us, not what ought to be in us. – C.S. Lewis, *Letters to Malcolm*

~

'Just what was going on in there, Marion? Stop and examine your actions!'

I sensed this clear moment of conviction as I was leaving a room in a Chinese orphanage. On paper, the words appear like a stern reprimand, but in fact they were a gentle prodding from God to reflect on my actions. To help you understand the significance of this moment – this moment when I was literally stopped in my tracks – I need to give some background information.

I strongly believe that all children are precious to God, that all children have a purpose and that all children can learn. As a teacher I have specialised in responding to students with learning disabilities in a range of contexts. I find great joy in seeing a child make small steps towards a learning goal. I have also had the privilege of nurturing many students with behavioural needs.

On this occasion, thanks to the generosity of a friend, I was visiting my husband in a large rural city in China. He was completing a six-month stay as a volunteer for a mission that, among other things, cared for abandoned babies. I had spent the first part of the morning of my visit to the orphanage in a big room with the toddlers, simply sitting on the floor of the poorly-resourced room, making myself available for lengthy cuddles, chit chat or a brief hug. Some infants sat with me for a matter of seconds, others spent longer. My two hours sitting there seemed such a simple contribution, yet the Chinese carer assigned to the room thanked me for helping prepare the hearts of the children to respond to their 'forever parents'. Most of the little ones in that room would one day be adopted by parents from the West.

Next I was taken to a small room where six or seven children were housed. These children were older and were not expected to be adopted. You see, they were all severely disabled. Either sitting in wheelchairs or lying on their beds, they were placed in a circle around the edge of the room. Along with the other visitors, I circuited the room three or four times, greeting each child, speaking words of love, holding a hand, smiling, stroking an arm, kissing a forehead. The room was bare and resources almost non-existent, but it was obvious the carers were genuine in their attention to the needs of these children.

It was as I left this room that God had spoken to my heart. I stopped and replayed each encounter in my mind. I had walked around the room, greeting each child at least three times. But had I? As I replayed my actions I realised I had bypassed one little girl every time – a child who appeared to be the most severely disabled.

I was shocked by my own behaviour. Why had I done this? I knew this girl was beautiful before God. I knew that Jesus would not ignore this precious life and that I must imitate Him. I confessed the dichotomy between my beliefs and actions, thankful for a merciful God.

I realised I was unsure of how to interact with the girl. Instead of facing my uncertainty and learning through interaction, I had shied away, giving in to my sense of inadequacy. God graciously grew my courage that day, in readiness for whatever new or daunting situation I would face next.

Deus peccata dimittit
(God forgives)

A Timely Lesson

If any of you lacks wisdom, you should ask God, who gives generously to all without finding fault, and it will be given to you. – James 1:5 (NIV)

If you don't know what you're doing, pray to the Father. He loves to help. You'll get his help, and won't be condescended to when you ask for it. Ask boldly, believingly, without a second thought. – James 1:5-8 (MSG)

~

It was almost the end of the semester and, in my role as a tertiary lecturer, I had journeyed with this group of trainee teachers for three years. I encouraged them to recall special moments and one student identified a particular teaching session from the first year. I remembered the occasion well.

We had been discussing literacy resources and I had explained my disappointment about the then-current Ready to Read series for young children because of the paucity of stories depicting nuclear families. A student had asked me to explain this further

– surely the range of family structures represented in these books was simply reflecting common family groupings in society?

Recognising that these 'common family groupings' were also present in our class, I realised that I would need to respond with empathy and wisdom, so I asked for a minute or two to pray about my response. This moment was what the student was recalling – for positive reasons – but the recollection left me feeling sad.

God had indeed guided my comments that day and a fruitful conversation had eventuated. So what was now causing my sadness? The fact that the student had recalled the *one (and only)* time I had stopped during class to pray for wisdom!

I was challenged to make this a regular practice rather than a memorable one-off event.

Dat sapientiam a Deo, ut qui
(God gives wisdom to those who ask)

God Guides My Pen

The only thing that matters is for each writer to hold fast unyieldingly the grace he personally receives and so fulfil perfectly his individual mission. – Athanasius, *On the Incarnation*

~

On occasions I think I have had a peep into the experience of the writers of scripture – a brief splinter of light into how they recorded God's Word. Not that I'm claiming to have written scripture! But I have definitely experienced God's hand on my pen.

The first occurrence was in Wuhan, China. A young pregnant woman told me she lacked knowledge about being a parent, since the breakdown between generations in China had meant her mother and grandmother had not been able to pass on their knowledge. She was fearful, worried that she might fail her child. I promised to prepare something for her overnight, as my husband and I were due to leave the next evening.

On returning to our hotel room I pondered, 'God, how can I communicate the key aspects of this vital role in a way that's clear, yet transcends language, culture and personal experiences? Please show me.'

Without further deliberation, I began mapping out a linear diagram based on five domains of development (physical, social, emotional, cognitive and spiritual), with two key responsibilities under each domain and then two practical ways to fulfil these under each responsibility.

The concepts flowed so readily that I knew it was the Holy Spirit's work. This was confirmed by the young woman's response as we talked through the diagram the next morning. She was overjoyed to receive practical ideas for her important role. I sometimes find myself wishing I had kept a copy, but then I remember that the chart was specifically given to meet the request of my young Chinese friend – it was a gift from God to her.

The second occurrence was in Tonga, where I was involved in facilitating learning experiences for pre-service student teachers. On my arrival, I was advised by a secondary principal that I would also, in several days time, lead a full professional development session with 60 staff members. I immediately rued the fact that I hadn't been told about this session before I left for Tonga, since at home I had many resources on which to draw. To add to the pressure, the principal expressed the hope that I might contribute to a shift towards Christian education being truly enacted in his school.

Trying to gather my thoughts in preparation, I was overwhelmed by responsibility as I sat before a blank piece of paper. My pen went to the lower right hand side of the page and my thoughts flowed so quickly I could barely keep up.

This time the diagram followed a circular pattern, moving from right to left, then up, and then left to right, back to where I had started. In the process I had covered certain key elements of teaching Christianly – namely, a teacher's knowledge, relationships, expectations, classroom environment, commitment, example and faith. I was fascinated by the way each section was interwoven, so that the image looked like brain connections. Each section led naturally into the next, then the final topic birthed the first; and each section was particularly relevant to the Tongan setting.

I delivered a one-hour talk based on this diagram in the heat of an outdoor evening. Afterwards, one staff member confided that it was the first time she had witnessed all staff members staying totally attentive to a topic being discussed for the full duration of the session. The hand of God was certainly on the material, and He had prepared the hearts of the audience to receive His instruction.

The principal asked if he could use the material in future staff meetings, taking one topic each week, and inviting staff to make personal responses. Of course I agreed. Even though I had developed the diagram – the material wasn't mine, it had been given for use in Tonga.

Spiritus Dei
(Breath of God)

Moonlight Enlightens

The heavens declare the glory of God; the skies proclaim the work of his hands. Day after day they pour forth speech; night after night they reveal knowledge. They have no speech, they use no words; no sound is heard from them. Yet their voice goes out into all the earth, their words to the ends of the world. – Psalm 19:1-4 (NIV)

~

One of my daughters gained a teaching position in the far north. This was cause for great celebration. The only downside was the distance between our home and her placement. When loneliness set in for her, I tried to visit as often as I could, making the six-hour excursion on Saturday morning with the six-hour return trip on Sunday night.

I enjoyed these journeys. Northland has such beautiful landscapes, with variety at every turn. The travel afforded me thinking time and opportunities to talk with God. However, these trips always came after busy weeks, and I was often tired, even before I left home.

One evening I was particularly weary on my return trip. The

darkening sky above me was wide and clear – not a cloud in sight. I was on a section of road that passed along the top of a ridge, winding with the contours of the land. As I drove I pretended the bright full moon was playing hide and seek with me. This may sound silly, but the game provided me with stimulation at a time when I needed it! Whenever I turned a corner, or moved past a large bush and the moon was revealed, I would exclaim, 'Got you!' Playing in this way brought me joy as I revelled in God's beautiful creation.

Imagine then my surprise when, on turning a corner, I found the moon was completely covered by a single black cloud, which seemed to have appeared out of nowhere. I was initially very cross, but then noticed a glowing ring around the entire cloud, a magnificent corona. Its beauty took my breath away, and dissipated my anger.

Then I felt God say, 'You see, Marion. The moon reflects the glory of the sun so brightly that even a dark cloud cannot completely dim its radiance. This is what I want for you too. Be so assured of your relationship with me, know me so well, that you reflect me. Then even when dark clouds appear in your day, my glory, my beauty will still emanate from you.'

What a challenge! At the next corner I saw the moon again, minus its black cloak, and once again in a cloudless sky.

That episode has remained with me ever since, and I continue to seek to grow into the fullness of Christ.

An Angel's Visitation

My God shall supply all my needs
According to His riches in glory
He will give His angels
Charge over me
Jehovah Jireh cares for me
– Don Moen, song lyric

~

I HAVE VISITED TONGA multiple times and have enjoyed a long association with the Free Wesleyan Education system, helping as part of a bilateral team equipping teachers in mission schools. My first night on Tongatapu, Tonga's main island, was spent in a small guest house. I never slept a wink.

First I lay in bed listening to the local church choir rehearsing for several hours. Almost immediately after they had finished for the night, the dogs started, as if to add their praises to those of the choir. The air was so still and clear that dogs could be heard all over the island, the kind of effect a surround sound system tries to replicate.

Once the dogs had quietened it was the turn of the pigs, free roaming and scavenging for tasty morsels, grunting as they explored. I was almost drifting off when, at 3.00 a.m., the roosters began to crow their strident wake-up call. By now I was wondering what would be next and found it difficult to settle. Would this descending quietness last? No! Next were the church bells at five, summoning people to arise in readiness for prayer. At 6.00 a.m. the hymn singing recommenced!

Fortunately it didn't take me long to adjust to the Tongan nightlife, and by the end of trip I was getting plenty of sleep.

During my next visit I stayed in a little house with several palangi (European) teachers, themselves new to Tonga. One evening we were invited to a prayer meeting at a residence further down the street, home to two elderly spinsters and their adult niece. The prayer group was attended by women intercessors, including a member of the royal family. These women prayed fervently for the needs of their families, communities and country. Even though we couldn't understand the prayers in Tongan, it was an inspiring experience.

For my third visit I was advised that I would be staying with a Tongan family who lived near the facility where I would be holding classes. I had already learned enough about Tongan culture to know that this was an unusual honour. While there is always an abundance of welcome, friendliness and generosity, it's not common for palangi to visit or stay in homes – unless time has allowed a genuine connection to be made.

Naturally I wondered how I would feel in this setting, and if I would recognise appropriate protocols. More importantly, I hoped I would not be an imposition, or cause the family to feel awkward. As I was driven from the airport to this unknown abode, I earnestly prayed that God would help me quickly find a point of connection, that I would find ways to demonstrate gratitude to the hosts and be perceptive of their feelings. I asked that they would readily accept me into their home and that I would feel at ease there.

I was still uttering this prayer when the van turned into the house that was to be my home for the next two weeks. Imagine my surprise when I realised it was the very house where I had attended the prayer meeting on the previous visit. It wasn't entirely unknown territory. Part of my prayer had already been answered.

On greeting the two elderly ladies, I reminded them of my presence at the prayer meeting several months earlier. We shared a few niceties and then I asked if I could rest for a while. I was shown to my room off the lounge, and was left to sleep for an hour or so.

When I awoke I was greeted with great excitement by the two sisters. It seemed that as I slept one of them had noticed an unknown stranger sitting in the lounge. She shared this with the other sister who suggested it was a figment of her imagination. A little later, on returning from the garden, the first sister again saw someone in the lounge. This time the description was so convincing she was believed, and the explanation given was that it was an angel checking to see that their house was suitable for me.

The women saw this as evidence that I was special to God. To them I was now a bone fide member of the family since I could be trusted, given that an angel was assessing the situation for me.

I stayed with this family at least ten times.

One of the sisters made it her mission to induct me as a Tongan. During each visit she would design challenges for me, to test how

'Tongan' I was becoming. On one occasion she sent me to the King's birthday luncheon (without an invitation), armed with a plastic bag in which I was to place food from the table. I returned to her with a bag full of fruit, meat and taro. I passed that test!

On another occasion she told me to wear a ceremonial faka'aveave into town. This is a plain, even rough, ceremonial 'skirt' made of dried pandanus leaves. It is worn at funerals, particularly for those of royal or noble birth. I knew the king had died three months earlier and I knew that funeral clothes were worn for extended periods of time depending on the importance of the person, or the closeness of the relationship. Duly dressed in the skirt, before setting out I checked once more that my hostess really wanted me to do this. She was determined, so I headed to town. No-one else was wearing this attire!

I felt quite awkward until a Tongan lady stopped me and said,

'Thank you for wearing your faka'aveave in honour of our late king. I have already ceased showing my respect and you, a palangi, are doing so. I feel ashamed.'

There were many more tests over several years before my host finally pronounced that I walked like a Tongan, ate like a Tongan and had good Tongan legs. Thereafter no further challenges were demanded.

Courage allowed me to learn and grow.

Building Blocks

What our free will is meant to do is help God write the story. – Madeleine L'Engle, *Walking on Water*

A gentle answer deflects anger, but harsh words make tempers flare. – Proverbs 15:1 (NLT)

~

I HAVE FULFILLED A number of roles in Tonga, such as presenting at a principal's retreat, leading professional learning sessions with tertiary lecturers, partnering with the Tongan Institute of Education to develop their first Diploma of Early Childhood programme and preaching at the English-speaking church.

However, my main involvement has been in helping to deliver a qualification for Tongan teachers in conjunction with the training institute I work for in New Zealand. This mission-based partnership sees New Zealand tutors leading block courses in Tonga at the beginning of each term for one or two weeks, with local tertiary educators guiding the students' study during the remainder of each term. The two-year diploma programme was first offered to unqualified teachers already in schools (known as 'in-service professional learning'). When all existing teachers had completed the diploma, the programme was offered to others who wanted to become teachers, including school leavers.

This change of focus is the background to my next story. I was teaching the first group of pre-service trainees, which included two particular school leavers. On the first day, we started into some relationship-building exercises. I learned that neither of these two students really wanted to be there. One attributed her attendance to the wishes of her mother. The other saw the programme as 'something to do to stop her being bored'. Both were obviously very capable, but they were disruptive, giggly and precocious.

One task required each student teacher to make an acrostic for his or her name. The two young ladies made a mockery of the task, putting silly descriptors beside each letter. I gently explained that tertiary study was a serious business and although we would at times have fun and laughter, this task was an occasion where they needed to provide sensible, informative responses. Surprised at being confronted, they moderated their behaviour somewhat. However, several other planned activities that morning also became avenues for tomfoolery.

In the afternoon, the programme I had planned involved asking the student teachers to read a potentially controversial article about skin colour. I was in two minds about using this reading, given that it might encourage flippant comments from the aforementioned young ladies. After praying, I decided to go ahead with the reading as originally planned. During the ensuing group discussion, one of the young ladies gave very articulate and insightful responses. God helped me recognise the gift of mercy within her, along with a passion for social justice.

After class I asked to speak to her privately. I commended her participation in the class discussion. I told her that God had shown me she had a gift of mercy. I mentioned social justice, which she asked me to explain. I explored with her the notion of speaking up for people who were disadvantaged. I told her that I believed God was calling her to be an advocate for such people.

The young lady looked at me in amazement – not because she doubted my words but because, she now told me, her true desire was to become a lawyer. She explained that her mother had advised her to train as a teacher first, as a way to grow the necessary skills to study law, and to teach for a few years to develop maturity in her interactions with others before continuing on the path to becoming a lawyer.

She was astonished that God would speak to her through me and was close to tears as she thanked me for sharing with her. She felt her plans had been affirmed. Thereafter she became totally committed to her study, fully participated in learning experiences and, although one of the youngest, exercised a degree of leadership in the class.

It was a great joy to see her complete her programme of study and take up a teaching position.

Unwell in Tonga

'Behold, God is my salvation; I will trust, and will not be afraid; for the L*ORD* *God is my strength and my song, and he has become my salvation.'* – Isaiah 12:2 (RSV)

I WAS CLEARLY UNWELL. Part way through my two-week stay in Tonga, this was not a welcome turn of events. I was required to teach for six hours the following day and, to compound matters, I had agreed to be observed by a visitor, an experienced teacher.

I went to bed early but my fitful sleep did nothing to enhance my wellbeing. I would awaken, at first unsure where I was, only to fall back into an unfulfilling state of drowsiness. Tonga had just beaten France in a Rugby World Cup match and the celebrations were raucous, but I had no energy or will to feel any joy over the nation's sporting success.

The next morning I felt no better. I sensed my fever had subsided but my body was heavy, sluggish and certainly not amenable to any enduring physical activity. As I wearily climbed the flight of stairs to the lecture room, I begged God to energise and equip me.

Without Him there was no way I would make it through the seven-hour day.

'Lord, I'm your servant, but today I lack the strength. Please be my strength. Please be my helper. Please cover my inadequacies. Give me energy. Help me journey with the students.'

And so the day began. Each time I felt weak, I internally reiterated my prayer, and we pressed on with the scheduled learning experiences. At the close of the day, as we packed up, the visitor who had been observing came to me.

'Marion, I've never seen such energy and enthusiasm in a teacher. It was wonderful to watch,' she said.

I quickly explained that what she had observed was the Holy Spirit in action, and gave thanks to God for answering my prayers. I bid the visitor farewell and returned to my bed!

Deus meus medicus
(God is my healer)

Speak Lord

For I will give you words and wisdom... – Luke 21:15 (NIV)

For my thoughts are not your thoughts and my ways are not your ways. – Isaiah 55:8 (NLV)

~

She stood before me, hesitant, a young Tongan woman with pleading eyes. It was the last day of the block course, after two weeks of full-day classes for those registered in the teaching programme. Everyone knew that full attendance was a compulsory component of the course. I was always particularly strong on this point.

She stood before me, holding out her question for my consideration. Could she join the study programme even though it was the last day of the course? Without a to or fro, without a why or wherefore, without a perhaps or maybe I heard myself say, 'Yes!'

I was as surprised as she was. How could this be? My tongue was speaking against my mind. Wondering what on earth was going on, I invited her to sit with the students, saying I would talk further with her later.

After class we met. She told me her name and then mentioned

that her father had been part of the programme the year before. I remembered him and immediately understood God's intervention – why I had been compelled to answer 'Yes'.

Her father, an older man, had shared with me his joy and thankfulness to God for the opportunity to gain new knowledge. A teacher for many years, at last he would be recognised as qualified. His delight in learning was obvious.

He then shared that his heart's desire was to see his precious daughter also complete the teaching programme sometime in the future.

It transpired that this man had unexpectedly passed away before that year was through, but here standing before me, six months later, was his precious daughter. Allowing the Holy Spirit to speak through me had begun the process of that father's dream becoming reality.

Cogitat enim Dei nostri bonam
(God plans for our good)

A Change of Plan

Take the first step in faith. You don't have to see the whole staircase, just take the first step. – Dr Martin Luther King Jr

~

'OH NO! WHAT'S GOING to happen now? Have I come all this way for nothing?'

I was excited to be visiting a refugee camp on the Thai-Burma border. I had often heard of the Karen people – a Christian ethnic minority within Myanmar – and knew that thousands of them had fled to Thai refugee camps to escape persecution.

I was also excited to be supporting a graduate from our institute in New Zealand, who was voluntarily spearheading an initiative among these strong people, training young adults to be teachers – hopefully within Karen State.

However, when I arrived in Chang-mai, I learned there was a significant 'challenge'. The new camp commandant, seeking to assert his authority, had banned all foreigners from visiting the camp. How would I be able to connect with the students? Where would classes be held?

A resourceful 'friend' of the programme arranged for the students to abscond from the camp, in the early hours of Monday morning, before the watchful guards had awakened. The students then walked for several hours through jungle to a traditional village, which was willing to house them for the week.

So class commenced that Monday morning with eager students, in a building without windows or doors, beside a small lake, in the vine-camouflaged village. God was in control of all things. Our week progressed as we forged relationships, connected our cultures, and explored God's Word, all while studying literacy and human development.

While I was working on my lesson plans for this teaching course before leaving New Zealand, God had impressed on my heart the need to be circumspect about the illustrations and stories I used in my teaching. He challenged me to avoid any example outside the experience of the Karen people, and to also use, as resources, only those materials to which they would have access.

That certainly proved to be a 'word of knowledge'. There was no electricity, no whiteboard, and not even a blackboard! Just prior to going to the village, I purchased basic resources such as paper and pens. As a last minute spontaneous decision, I also bought a flip chart I had noticed in the corner of the crammed shop, thinking it might be useful as art paper, but which, because of the unexpected change of venue, became our 'record of learning'.

On the third day, as I contentedly watched the students engage in an activity, I mentioned to a colleague, 'I feel right at home here.' At first he thought I was offering to stay long term! I quickly explained that what I meant was I knew I was in exactly the right place for that time, doing exactly the right thing for exactly the right reason. I felt surrounded by God's love and grace.

God had everything in control. The students and I ended up working in an environment that was much more pleasant than the refugee camp, and God used an egotistical camp commandant to bring that to pass. Another whiff of God's sense of humour!

Deus est fidelis
(God is faithful)

A Tiny Theophany

To receive a pleasure and to recognise its divine source are a single experience. To experience the tiny theophany is itself to adore ... These pure and spontaneous pleasures are 'patches of Godlight' in the woods of our experience.
– C.S. Lewis, *Letters to Malcolm*

~

Noh Bo (Thai-Burma border)

In the early morning hour
Cool
Freshly fallen rain water
Spills over the concrete barrel
Housed within a ramshackle enclosure

In my hand a simple pot
Dips
Without a ripple
Emerging full and ready
To bathe my body then dip again

A strangely sacred action
Beyond words

– Marion

Pride Goes Before a Fall

Close the book gently and close it with prayer.
– My Nana

I WAS DELIGHTED TO be asked to mentor a new staff member at the tertiary institute where I work, and quickly formed a connection with her, especially as a prayer partner. Quite soon after being introduced, she asked to observe one of my teaching sessions, explaining she had heard I used scripture effectively in my discussions. I confess to feeling a hint of pride, but I was also a tad relieved because I had actually prepared to use scripture in a teaching session the next day. I invited my new friend to join my literacy class, where we would be discussing the importance of helping children learn how to read.

My plan was to discuss the incident recorded in Daniel 5, where King Belshazzar was perplexed by the writing on the wall. I would point out that it was not seeing the hand writing on the wall that caused him to go pale and have his legs give way, since magical acts were common in his day. Rather it was the fact that he couldn't read the writing. He was desperate to know what it said. I then planned to use this Biblical story as a way into discussing reading difficulties for children.

I began the lesson by reading the first seven verses, then, in the interest of time, missed out the next five lengthy verses that I felt didn't add anything significant to the story. I chanted, 'Dum-de-dum-de-dum,' as I ran my finger down to verse 13, where I again picked up the story. The session went well, the students seemed to get the point and my colleague thanked me for the demonstration, adding kind words of encouragement.

But all was not well that night as I sat with God to review the day.

'So what was with the 'dum-de-dum'?' He asked. 'Isn't every part of my Word there for your edification? Isn't every part important? And if you are using selected verses, at least do so with decorum and respect.'

I realised I hadn't honoured God's Word in the way I should. I had treated it lightly, in the midst of my moment of pride, and thereby modelled a poor example to my students.

I sought God's forgiveness and the next day I apologised to my class and to my visiting colleague.

A Practical God

This is God*'s Word on the subject: ...I know what I'm doing. I have it all planned out – plans to take care of you, not abandon you, plans to give you the future you hope for.*
– Jeremiah 29:10-11 (MSG)

~

Approaching practicum was always a time of tension, trust, uncertainty, excitement, trepidation and hope – not just for the student teachers, but for me as well. For many years I had the task of placing the primary student teachers in classrooms for extended 'field work' opportunities. I always prayed about such placements, and considered each student teacher separately, desiring to find the 'perfect match' based on personality, student teacher strengths, associate teacher, school, location and so on.

It was part of my responsibility to ensure that the student teachers experienced a range of contexts: rural/urban, state/integrated, junior/middle/senior, low/high decile, to name a few. We needed to be able to assure the officials at the Teachers Council that all our graduates were equipped to teach in any New Zealand primary school.

So you can see that organising placements was a high-responsibility task, and you can also see why I felt the need to pray over every placement. God was so faithful in this process. Often students would later comment that their placement was 'perfect'. Even those who had a more difficult time were able to see what God had grown in them during the practicum.

One student was particularly nervous about going on her first placement. She had emigrated from South Africa a few years previously, and was unsure about being in a New Zealand primary school, having never experienced one herself. I prayed, and felt that I should place her with a teacher I actually didn't know. This was quite unusual, as I made every effort to build connections with the associates who provided practicum placements for our students. However, I knew the school was very supportive of its teachers, and with nothing else that seemed suitable, the arrangement was confirmed. Imagine my delight when I learned the associate teacher was also from South Africa!

Another student (a mature family man who, with his wife, often fostered children) needed a final placement and the practicum start date was only a week away. In this practicum students were required to exercise full responsibility for a class over a period of weeks. Obviously a good match was advantageous – in fact the final practicum, although in July/August, was always the first one I organised at the beginning of each year.

Yet somehow this student was without an agreed placement. I assured him I had committed the situation to God in prayer, and that all would be well. Time passed, and soon he was the only one of his cohort not yet on practicum. Another day passed and then another. Finally, four days later, a placement became available – with a male teacher of the same ethnicity, in a class of boys who needed a lot of love and guidance from a male role model, teaching in a language in which the student teacher was fluent! He was overwhelmed by God's goodness and so was I.

God as Teacher

God's future is arriving in the present, in the person and work of Jesus, and you can practise, right now, the habits of life which will find their goal in that coming future.
– Tom Wright, *Virtue Reborn*

~

I WAS INVITED TO present a paper at a teacher educator conference in China. What an experience! It started off so well. I arrived at Beijing Airport in the evening. My bag was one of the last to appear on the baggage carousel (as usual), but I quickly found the 'Line 4' bus.

It was already dark, and the lights of the city gave me fleeting views of the environment. I sat next to a young man who spoke English, and he guided me to the correct stop at which to alight. But then, where to? I had glimpsed the hotel sign from the bus, but once I crossed the overpass, the sign was no longer in view.

As I lugged my heavy suitcase down the overpass steps, another man offered to help. When I asked directions to Friendship Hotel he simply said, 'Follow me!' So follow I did, as he proceeded to guide me, all the while speaking in perfect English.

After quite a long walk, he delivered me to the main building. Frank (as he introduced himself) was an 'angel' sent by God. The Friendship Hotel was, in fact, a mini-village, with more than 10 high-rise buildings. Trying to orientate myself in the dark, without Frank's help, might have proven to be more than this weary traveller could manage.

The next day, my second challenge soon presented itself. All my previous communications regarding the conference had indicated hour-long sessions for the presentations. I had diligently prepared, only to discover that presenters had, in fact, now been allocated just 20 minutes speaking time. I hastily made some major adjustments to my material and the expectation of needing some fast talking to cover my material turned out to be 'a word of knowledge', as I will now explain.

I was scheduled to be the second speaker in a session running from 8.30 a.m. to midday. The Chinese educator taking the Chair seemed unfamiliar with English. We were late starting, probably at least 10 minutes.

The first presenter was a Turkish educator speaking in English about teaching German to Turkish students. He kept to his 20-minute timeframe, after which the Chair thanked him by talking about friends he (the Chair) had in Turkey and praising Turkey for being the bridge between the East and the West.

Then it was my turn. I saw our Chair check the printed presentation schedule, and then look at his watch. He seemed to have forgotten that we had started late. I was presenting a paper based on my research into barriers faced by Tongan students studying in New Zealand, with particular emphasis on 'encouragement of the heart'.

And so I began. Just 10 minutes into my presentation, the

Chair gesticulated that I should 'move along', and reinforced this at 12 minutes. My main points were very hurried, even poorly presented. I gave in to his pressure and cut my presentation short by at least six minutes. The Chair thanked me for the blue sea and blue sky of New Zealand.

I returned to my seat, feeling disappointed and concerned that I had let down those in New Zealand who had sent me, and wasted scarce finances – so much money to travel from New Zealand to China to give a 13-minute garbled talk!

Then the next speaker began his presentation (in Chinese)… 10 minutes… 15 minutes… 20 minutes… 25 minutes… 30 minutes. I sensed a range of unfamiliar feelings emerge in me – annoyance, frustration, offence, anger. Tears welled up and I absented myself from the room for a few minutes. We had been told to be present for a question and answer session at the end of the morning, so I returned and persevered, trying to hide my sense of disequilibrium.

Another Chinese academic took the podium, also for 30 minutes, and then others followed – none of whom I understood as I hadn't been provided with an interpreter. The Chair responded in full to each speaker, and also accepted lengthy comments from the floor.

Throughout the morning I had been journaling events and at this stage I wrote:

> This experience feels demoralising, it feels ostracising, it feels lonely, it feels minority…

> …it feels like God is giving me the opportunity to experience first-hand what I earlier talked about in my

presentation – cultural difference as a site of struggle, a repressive, restricting, emotional place.

In His wisdom, God had provided me with a living object lesson, a practical, personal experience of the focus of my research. When I had stood up to speak, I had known my material from an academic perspective – now I knew it at a deeply personal, emotional level as well. God is a great teacher!

Prudentia de Deus
(God gives insight)

God is Trustworthy

Spiritual formation... is a process of increasingly being possessed and permeated by spiritual fruit as we walk in the easy yoke of discipleship with Jesus our teacher ... We were meant to be inhabited by God and to live by a power beyond ourselves. – Dallas Willard, *The Great Omission*

~

I WAS INVITED TO lead an initiative in a large international school in China, with the goal of establishing a coaching culture within the staff. It was hoped that teachers would benefit from the support and accountability that could come from applying coaching skills in their interactions with each other. The teachers and students at this school represented many nationalities, but were mainly British, Canadian, Australian and New Zealanders. As with most international schools, product, outputs, exam results and academic standing were very important – sometimes to the detriment of the wellbeing of teachers. It was hoped that a coaching culture would offer support, encouragement and professional learning to staff.

But rather than talk about the development of the programme,

I want to share an aspect of what I learned from this process.

Before my first visit, I thought about how I might provide a Christian witness in this non-religious school environment. It was a place where I would not have the freedom to talk about Jesus in the way I did in my own workplace. I prayed earnestly that somehow, in this atheistic country, and in this secular school, I would be able to demonstrate Christ's influence in my life. I really wanted my words, actions and interactions to come from a place of holiness. I wanted to practise the presence of Christ, and I begged God that somehow He would be seen in my life.

In my role as a consultant to the school, I was afforded the privilege of planning as I went. I wasn't required to present an overview of how my contributions would develop over time. During my visits, I interacted with a number of teachers in a series of workshops. In between visits, I waited on God for directions regarding the content of the next set of workshops. He showed me the crucial need to pay attention to the wellbeing of staff, and gave me ideas about how to do that through the workshops. He also gave me the courage to be very direct with those leading the school when I was assessing the health of the organisation. These conversations were well received as God guided my words and the examples I drew upon.

I also had the unique experience of sitting in on the conversations of coaching pairs, then giving feedback to the novice coach. During the first three visits, I listened in on over 60 such conversations. It was an amazing privilege to be part of this process, and I gained a unique view of the 'inner workings' of the school.

But I was still asking God, 'Am I demonstrating Christ? Are people aware of Him as they interact with me? How could I know?'

At the end of my fourth visit, the headmaster drew me aside

and said, 'Marion, I'd like to invite you to come for another year, to continue developing this coaching programme. I've introduced a number of new initiatives in the last three years and this is the only one that teachers have not complained about!'

I tended to think that the teachers had given the programme a positive reception because it was about them and their well-being, rather than because of anything I had done, but then he continued…

'Marion, you have an ability I don't have. My staff all trust you as soon as they meet you.'

My question had been answered – all thanks and praise to God. I believed the deeper truth was that Christ's presence in me had opened up a sense of trust, because Christ is trustworthy. While no-one mentioned Christ, I knew He had been present as I worked alongside those teachers.

I felt incredibly humbled and excited. God is so faithful. As long as I actively seek His presence, He will guide my decision-making, my teaching and my witness.

Deus autem nobiscum
(God is with us)

Epilogue

Wherever He may guide me,
No want shall turn me back;
My Shepherd is beside me,
And nothing can I lack.
His wisdom ever waketh,
His sight is never dim;
He knows the way He taketh,
And I will walk with Him.
– Anna Waring, 'In Heavenly Love Abiding'

~

THE VIGNETTES IN THIS book represent just a handful of the times when God has, over many years, intervened in my teaching life. There are countless more examples, but these were the ones He brought to my mind to share.

As I reread the stories, I'm incredibly humbled by the gentle and gracious way God has led me, even when He has needed to correct me. He has used 'circumstances' to increase my understanding of what a Christian teacher thinks, says and does.

I know there is still more to learn, and I'm very willing to carry on following His lead.

I believe God wants to intervene, support and enrich every person's work – whether that be law, medicine, retail, fire-fighting, clerical, accountancy, homemaking, social work or teaching. I think you get my point. Whatever work we do, when we do it 'as to the Lord', He will guide, instruct and equip us, to His glory.

When friends and colleagues asked me to write these memoirs, at first I was daunted. I embarked on a retreat to see if God would give me guidance about what to write, to see if He would bring instances to my mind, as I'm not so good at recalling things from the past. I left the retreat with 14 ideas. By the time I finished this book I had 31.

Writing these stories has caused my heart to overflow with joy and thankfulness, for God is indeed a good leader and teacher – very good indeed!

Memoir n. (Fr. *memoire,* L. *memoria,* memory). A record of something noteworthy. Events recollected. Circa 1670

Vignette n. (Fr. *vigne, L. Vinea,* a vine). A literary sketch or description. Circa 1880

Intervene v. (L. *intervenire,* go between). Be between, mediate, interrupt. Circa 1640

References

Quotes

C.S. Lewis (1964, p. 75). *Letters to Malcolm*. New York, NY: Harvest Books

Mary Anne Radmacher www.goodreads.com/author/quotes/149829.Mary_Anne_Radmacher

Oswald Chambers www.goodreads.com/author/quotes/41469.Oswald_Chambers

Billy Graham www.goodreads.com/author/quotes/40328.Billy_Graham

Leslie Brandt (1983, p. 144). *Psalms Now.* Adelaide, Australia: Lutheran Publishers.

Madeleine L'Engle (1980, p. 51). *Walking on Water*. New York, NY: Farrar, Strauss and Giroux.

hooks, bell. (1993, p. 148). bell hooks speaking about Paulo Friere – the man, his work. In P. McLaren and P. Leanard (Eds.). *Paulo Freire: A critical encounter*. London, UK: Routledge.

C.S. Lewis (1964, p. 22). *Letters to Malcolm*. New York, NY: Harvest Books

St Athanasius (296-373 AD) (1982, p. 103). *On the Incarnation*. Translated by a religious of CSMV. London, England: Mowbray.

Don Moen www.azlyrics.com/lyrics/donmoen/jehovahjireh.html

Madeleine L'Engle (1980, p. 105). *Walking on Water*. New York, NY: Farrar, Strauss and Giroux.

Dr Martin Luther King www.goodreads.com/quotes/199214

C.S. Lewis (1964, p. 89, 91). *Letters to Malcolm*. New York, NY: Harvest Books

Tom Wright (2010, p. 90). *Virtue Reborn*. London, United Kingdom: SPCK.

Dallas Willard (2006, p. 16, 17). *The Great Omission*. San Francisco, LA: HarperCollins

Bible versions

www.ingramcontent.com/pod-product-compliance
Ingram Content Group UK Ltd.
Pitfield, Milton Keynes, MK11 3LW, UK
UKHW040027200726
13854UKWH00001B/395

9 780473 436599